Design: Art of Design
Recipe Photography: Peter Barry
Jacket and Illustration Artwork: Jane Winton, courtesy
of Bernard Thornton Artists, London
Editors: Jillian Stewart and Kate Cranshaw

CLB 3523
Published by Grange Books, an imprint of Grange Books
PLC, The Grange, Grange Yard, London, SE1 3AG
© 1994 CLB Publishing, Godalming, Surrey, England.
Printed and bound in Singapore
Published 1994
ISBN 1-85627-464-0

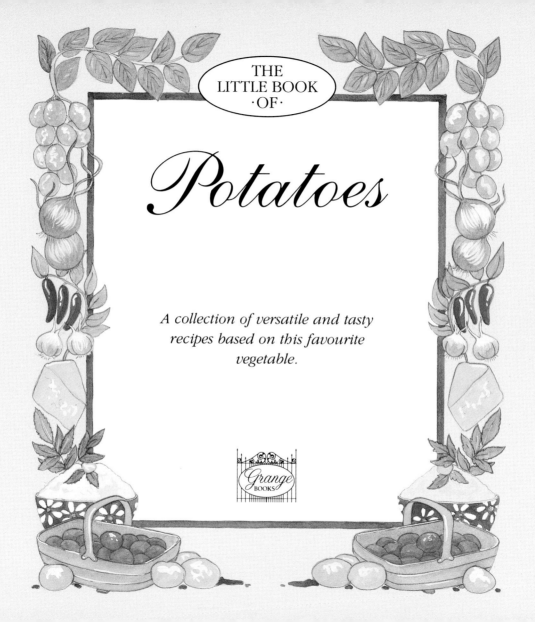

THE LITTLE BOOK ·OF·

Potatoes

A collection of versatile and tasty recipes based on this favourite vegetable.

Grange BOOKS

Introduction

Native to South America, the potato was encountered there by the Spanish invaders and subsequently introduced into Europe in the 16th century. At first, being new and scarce, they were food only for the rich. By the 19th century, however, they became widely available, and indeed the poorer people ate little else, to the extent that when potato blight hit Ireland from 1845 to 1851, the resultant famine caused the death of over a million Irish people.

There are dozens of different varieties of potato, each with its own characteristics. There are subtle taste variations between types, and significant differences in texture, ranging from the firm-fleshed, waxy varieties, such as the Maris Bard, which are so delicious when boiled with a sprig of mint and served hot with butter or cold in salads, to the disintegrating, mealy types, such as the Russet, which are perfect for baking, mashing and pureeing.

For flavour, there is nothing to compare with new potatoes. These are dug in early spring, while still small and sweet, and they have a high vitamin C content. They should be eaten fresh, and not stored for longer than 48 hours, after which their texture and flavour tend to deteriorate. Their skins are damp and rub off easily, and they need only to be scrubbed clean before being cooked. They are at their best just boiled.

Mature potatoes are harvested from September to October, once their green tops have died and their sugar content has been converted into starch. Stored in a cool, dry, dark place, they will keep well for several weeks, or even months.

Some people like to peel their potatoes, while others love the flavour and 'bite' of the skins left on. If you peel them, then do so thinly, as much of the goodness and the vitamins lie just beneath the skin.

It is hard to think of a cooking method that cannot be used for the preparation of potatoes. We boil them, fry them, bake them, steam them, mash them and curry them. The advent of the microwave oven has greatly popularised the baked potato as a quick and nourishing lunch or supper dish. Potatoes are easy to grow, and even improve the soil. They are cheap to buy, and are wonderfully filling – in short, the potato is a most obliging, versatile and popular food.

Potatoes are not eaten raw and are rarely used in desserts, but otherwise there are endless possibilities for this humble but incredibly versatile vegetable. It thickens soups, fills pancakes, deliciously absorbs flavours in curries and stews, and can be whipped, chipped and fashioned into any number of attractive shapes. Glance through the imaginative recipes in these pages to discover something of the potato's tremendous culinary potential.

Potato Cakes

SERVES 6-8

These fried potato cakes make a delicious snack or side dish.

PREPARATION: 15 mins
COOKING: 6 mins

120g/4oz plain flour
½ tsp salt
½ tsp baking powder
30g/1oz butter
900g/2lbs mashed potato
Bacon fat or oil

---

1. Sift the flour, salt and baking powder into a mixing bowl. Rub in the butter until evenly blended.

2. Mix in the mashed potatoes and knead the mixture into a ball.

3. Cut the potato mixture in half and roll out each bit, on a floured board or work surface, into a circle about 1.25cm/½-inch thick. Divide each circle into four segments.

4. Heat a griddle or heavy-based frying pan until very hot. Add a little bacon fat or oil to the pan and slide in some of the potato cakes. Cook for 2-3 minutes on each side until hot and browned.

Potato Soup

SERVES 8-10

Potatoes make a tasty and hearty soup which requires no thickening.

PREPARATION: 15 mins
COOKING: 1 hr

900g/2lbs potatoes
2 medium onions
1 small carrot
60g/2oz butter
1.14 litre/2 pints stock
570ml/1 pint milk
Bay leaf, thyme and parsley
Salt and pepper
Cream and chives, for garnish

1. Peel and slice the potatoes, onions and carrot. Melt butter in a large saucepan and sauté the onions in it until soft but not brown.

2. Add the potatoes and carrot. Stir in the stock and milk.

3. Tie the bay leaf, thyme and parsley together, and add to the pan, along with salt and pepper to taste.

4. Simmer gently for about 1 hour then either blend or put through a sieve or vegetable mill.

5. Add some cream before serving and sprinkle with chopped chives.

Potatoes with Garlic and Chillies

SERVES 4-6

These are rather like spicy French fries, but they are not deep fried.

PREPARATION: 15-20 mins
COOKING: 15 mins

460g/1lb potatoes, peeled and washed
3 tbsps cooking oil
½ tsp black mustard seeds
½ tsp cumin seeds
4 cloves garlic, crushed
¼-½ tsp chilli powder
½ tsp ground turmeric
1 tsp salt or to taste

1. Cut the potatoes to the thickness of French fries, but half their length.

2. In a large non-stick or cast iron frying pan, heat the oil over a medium heat.

3. Add the mustard seeds and then the cumin. When the seeds start popping, add the garlic and allow it to lightly brown.

4. Remove the pan from the heat and stir in the chilli powder and turmeric.

5. Add the potatoes and place the pan back on the heat. Stir and turn up the heat to medium.

6. Add the salt, stir and mix, then cover the pan and cook for 3-4 minutes and stir again. Continue to do this until the potatoes are cooked through and lightly browned. Remove from the heat.

Pommes Dauphiné

SERVES 6

This dish from the mountainous province of France is robust fare.

PREPARATION: 25 mins
COOKING: 30-40 mins

1 clove garlic, crushed
30g/1oz butter
1kg/2¼lbs potatoes, peeled and thinly sliced
175g/6oz grated Comté or Gruyère cheese
Salt and pepper
90g/3oz butter cut into very small dice
140ml/¼ pint single cream

1. Rub the bottom and sides of a heavy baking dish with the crushed clove of garlic. Grease the bottom and sides liberally with the butter.

2. Spread half of the potato slices in the bottom of the dish, sprinkle with half the cheese, some salt and pepper and dot with half the butter. Top with the remaining slices of potato, neatly arranged. Sprinkle with the

Step 2 Layer the potatoes with the cheese and seasoning.

remaining cheese, salt and pepper and butter.

3. Pour in the cream down the inside of the dish around the potatoes.

4. Cook in the top part of an oven preheated to 200°C/400°F/Gas Mark 6, for 30-40 minutes, or until the potatoes are tender and the top is nicely browned. Serve immediately.

Step 1 Rub the dish with garlic and butter it well.

Step 3 Pour in the cream down the inside of the dish.

Hot Potato Salad with Bacon

SERVES 6-8

If Germany has a national salad this must be it. It is perfect with any of the country's many varieties of sausage.

PREPARATION: 25 mins
COOKING: 35 mins

6-8 even-sized potatoes (waxy variety)
Pinch salt
120g/4oz smoked streaky bacon, diced
1 onion
140ml/¼ pint white wine vinegar
140ml/¼ pint water or beef stock
3 tbsps soured cream (optional)
Salt and pepper
2 tbsps chopped parsley

---

1. Boil the potatoes in their jackets in lightly salted water to cover. When they are just tender,

Step 2 Follow the natural lines in the onion and make vertical cuts through the onion nearly to the root end.

Step 2 Cut the onion crosswise into large or small pieces as needed.

drain and peel while still hot. Cut into thin slices and place in a serving dish.

2. Fry the bacon in a large frying pan. Meanwhile, chop the onion very finely. Once the bacon is pale golden add the onion and continue to sauté slowly until transparent but not brown.

3. Remove the pan from the heat and gradually pour in the vinegar and the water or stock. Bring to the boil and remove from the heat.

4. Stir in the soured cream, if using, and pour the mixture over the potatoes. Lift the potatoes so that the dressing runs over them evenly. Sprinkle with salt and pepper and parsley. Serve immediately.

Pommes Noisettes

SERVES 4-6

These delicious cheesy potato balls will complement any meal, from a sophisticated dinner party to a family meal.

PREPARATION: 15 mins, plus chilling
COOKING: 30 mins

460g/1lb potatoes, peeled and cut into chunks
30g/1oz butter or vegetable margarine
Salt and freshly ground black pepper
60g/2oz Gruyère or Edam cheese, finely grated
60g/2oz ground hazelnuts
Oil for shallow frying
Fresh parsley or watercress sprigs, to garnish

---

1. Cook the potatoes in boiling salted water until tender then drain and mash well.

2. Add the butter or margarine, seasoning and cheese and fork through until well combined then refrigerate until completely cold.

3. Shape spoonfuls of the cold mashed potato into 2.5cm/1-inch balls.

Step 3 Shape spoonfuls of the refrigerated mashed potato into balls approximately 2.5cm/1 inch in diameter.

4. Spread the nuts on a plate and roll the potato balls in the nuts, making sure they are well coated.

5. Heat the oil in a large frying pan and sauté the potato until golden, turning frequently until they are lightly browned and crisp.

6. Serve garnished with parsley or watercress.

Aloo Ki Bhaji

SERVES 4-6

Boiled potatoes, diced and braised with a few whole spices and onions make a quick and easy side dish.

PREPARATION: 35-45 mins
COOKING: 20 mins

680g/1½lbs potatoes
75-90ml/5-6 tbsps cooking oil
½ tsp black mustard seeds
2-3 dried red chillies
⅛ tsp fenugreek (methi) seeds
225g/8oz onions, finely sliced
1-2 fresh green chillies, sliced lengthwise (and deseeded if wished)
1 tsp ground turmeric
1 tsp salt or to taste
30g/1oz chopped coriander leaves

---

1. Boil the potatoes in their jackets and allow to cool thoroughly.

2. Peel the potatoes and dice them evenly.

3. Heat the oil in a large frying pan over a medium heat, add the mustard seeds and fry until they pop.

4. Add the dried red chillies and the fenugreek seeds, then immediately follow with the onions and the fresh green chillies.

5. Fry the onions for 8-10 minutes, or until they are golden brown.

6. Add the turmeric, potatoes and salt. Stir and fry gently for another 8-10 minutes, until the potatoes are heated through.

7. Remove from heat and stir in the coriander leaves.

Potato Whip

This is an excellent way of using up left over mashed potatoes, and making them taste just as good, if not better than when they were first cooked!

PREPARATION: 10 mins
COOKING: 30 mins

30g/1oz butter or margarine
680g/1½lbs cold mashed potatoes
60ml/4 tbsps hot milk
2 eggs, separated
Freshly grated nutmeg
Salt and pepper
60g/2oz grated cheese

---

1. Melt the butter and beat it into the cold mashed potatoes together with the hot milk and egg yolks. Season well with the nutmeg, salt and pepper.

2. Whisk the egg whites until stiff and fold them gently but thoroughly into the potato mixture.

3. Pile the mixture into a baking dish and smooth the top level. Sprinkle over the grated cheese and bake in an oven preheated to 200°C/400°F/Gas Mark 6, for about 30 minutes, or until the cheese topping is nicely browned and the potato mixture piping hot.

Potato and Chestnut Hot-Pot

SERVES 4-6

This enticing hot-pot is ideal for a vegetarian meal if served with a lightly cooked green vegetable.

PREPARATION: 20 mins
COOKING: 1¼ hrs

680g/1½ lbs potatoes
3 medium onions
225g/8oz brown lentils
225g/8oz fresh chestnuts, shelled and peeled
Salt and pepper
420ml/¾ pint warm stock
60g/2oz butter or margarine

---

1. Peel and slice the potatoes and onions thinly.

2. Put layers of potatoes, onions, lentils and chestnuts into a greased pie dish ending with a layer of potatoes.

3. Season well between each layer and pour over the warm stock.

4. Dot with margarine and cover. Bake in an oven preheated to 190°C/375°F/Gas Mark 5 for 1 hour or until the potatoes are tender.

5. Turn up the oven to 200°C/400°F/Gas Mark 6, remove the lid from the casserole and return to the oven for 10-15 minutes until the potatoes are crispy and golden brown on top.

Colcannon

This classic Irish potato dish is wonderful served with boiled ham.

PREPARATION: 10 mins
COOKING: 15 mins

60g/2oz butter
120g/4oz finely chopped onion, leek or
   spring onion
60ml/4 tbsps milk
460g/1lb cooked mashed potatoes
340g/12oz cooked cabbage

1. Heat the butter in a pan until foaming. Add the onion, leek or spring onions and sauté until soft.

2. Add the milk and the well-mashed potatoes and stir until heated through.

3. Chop the cabbage finely and beat into the mixture over a low heat until all the mixture is pale green and fluffy.

Nutty Potato Cakes

MAKES 8 CAKES

Serve these delicious cakes with grilled meat or fish and salad.

PREPARATION: 10 mins
COOKING: 25 mins

460g/1lb potatoes
15g/½oz butter or margarine
A little milk
90g/3oz mixed nuts, finely ground
30g/1oz sunflower seeds, finely ground
2 tbsps finely chopped spring onions
Salt and freshly ground black pepper
Flour for coating
Oil for frying

1. Peel the potatoes, cut into pieces and boil until just soft.

2. Drain and mash with the butter and milk to a creamy consistency.

3. Add the nuts, seeds, spring onions and salt and pepper to taste.

4. If necessary, add a little more milk at this stage to give a soft texture which holds together.

5. Divide the mixture into 8 and shape into cakes using wet hands.

6. Coat the cakes with flour and fry quickly in a little oil. Drain on kitchen paper and serve immediately.

Perfect Potatoes

SERVES 4-6

Potatoes become extra special when teamed up with the flavour of onion.

PREPARATION: 15 mins
COOKING: 1-1½ hrs

900g/2lbs potatoes
1 large onion
Salt and pepper
280ml/½ pint milk
45g/1½oz butter or margarine

1. Peel and finely slice the potatoes and onion.

2. Layer the potato slices and onion in a shallow ovenproof dish, sprinkling each layer with some salt and pepper.

3. Pour over the milk and dot with the butter or margarine.

4. Bake uncovered in an oven preheated to 180°C/350°F/Gas Mark 4 for 1-1½ hours or until the potatoes are soft, golden and brown on top.

Bavarian Potato Salad

SERVES 4-6

It is best to prepare this salad a few hours in advance to allow the potatoes to absorb the flavours. Serve with cold roasts.

PREPARATION: 15 mins
COOKING: 15 mins

900g/2lbs tiny new potatoes
60ml/4 tbsps olive oil
4 spring onions, finely chopped
1 clove garlic, crushed
2 tbsps fresh dill, chopped or 1 tbsp dried
2 tbsps wine vinegar
½ tsp sugar
Seasoning
2 tbsps chopped fresh parsley

1. Wash the potatoes but do not peel. Put them into a pan, cover with cold water and some salt and boil until just tender.

2. Whilst the potatoes are cooking, heat the olive oil in a frying pan and cook the spring onions and garlic for 2-3 minutes until they have softened a little.

3. Add the dill and cook gently for a further minute.

4. Add the wine vinegar and sugar, and stir until the sugar dissolves. Remove from the heat and add a little seasoning.

5. Drain the potatoes and pour the dressing over them whilst they are still hot.

6. Allow to cool and sprinkle with the chopped parsley before serving.

Watercress Stuffed Potatoes

SERVES 4

An unusual and tasty way of serving baked potatoes.

PREPARATION: 20 mins
COOKING: 1¼ hours

4 large baking potatoes, scrubbed
4 eggs
60g/2oz butter or margarine
120g/4oz button mushrooms, sliced
1 shallot, peeled and finely chopped
45g/1½oz plain flour
420ml/¾ pint milk
60g/2oz Cheddar cheese, grated
Pinch dry mustard and cayenne pepper
Salt and freshly ground black pepper
1 bunch watercress, finely chopped

1. Prick the potatoes a few times with a fork and place them directly on the shelf of an oven preheated to 200°C/400°F/Gas Mark 6. Bake for ¾-1 hour, depending on the size, or until they are soft when squeezed. Reduce the temperature to 160°C/325°F/Gas Mark 3 and keep warm whilst completing the dish.

2. Poach the eggs in gently simmering water for 3½-5 minutes until the white and yolk are set. Remove from the pan and keep in cold water until required.

3. Melt 15g/½oz of the butter in a small pan and sauté mushrooms and shallot for about 5 minutes until softened.

4. Melt the remaining butter in a saucepan, stir in the flour and cook for 1 minute. Remove from the heat and gradually stir in 280ml/½ pint of the milk. Return to the heat and cook gently until thickened. Add the cheese and stir until it melts. Season with the mustard, cayenne, salt and pepper.

5. Cut a slice off the top of each potato and scoop out the flesh leaving a border inside each skin to form a firm shell.

6. Put equal amounts of the mushroom mixture into each shell and top with an egg. Spoon the cheese sauce over the top.

7. Scald the remaining milk, mash the potato flesh, then gradually beat in the hot milk and watercress. Pipe or spoon the potato over the sauce in the potato shell. Sprinkle the top with a little extra cheese and return to the oven for 15 minutes to warm through.

Kashmiri Dum Aloo

SERVES 4

This Indian dish of boiled potatoes fried until golden then simmered in yogurt and spices is a lovely way to serve new potatoes.

PREPARATION: 30-35 mins
COOKING: 20-25 mins

570g/1¼lbs small new potatoes, scrubbed
2 tbsps ghee or unsalted butter
1 tsp fennel seeds

Mix the following 5 ingredients in a small bowl

½ tsp ground cumin
1 tsp ground coriander
¼ tsp freshly ground black pepper
½ tsp ground turmeric
½ tsp ground ginger

150g/5oz thick set natural yogurt
1 tsp salt or to taste
¼ tsp garam masala
1 tbsp chopped coriander leaves
1 fresh green chilli, seeded and finely chopped

---

1. Boil the potatoes in their jackets, cool and peel them. Prick the potatoes all over with a cocktail stick to enable the spices to flavour them thoroughly.

2. Melt the ghee over a medium heat in a non-stick or cast-iron frying pan.

3. When the ghee is hot, fry the potatoes in a single layer for 8-10 minutes, or until they are browned, turning them over frequently. Remove them with a slotted spoon and set aside.

4. Remove the pan from the heat and stir in the fennel seeds followed by the spice mixture. Place the pan back over a low heat, stir the spices and fry for 1 minute.

5. Add the yogurt and salt, and mix well. Add the potatoes, cover the pan and simmer for 10-12 minutes. Stir in the garam masala and remove the pan from the heat.

6. Stir in the coriander leaves and the green chilli.

Boxty Pancakes

SERVES 4-6

These pancakes, made from both cooked and raw potatoes, can also be flavoured with some chopped herbs, onion or caraway seeds.

PREPARATION: 15 mins
COOKING: 15 mins

225g/8oz raw potatoes
225g/8oz cooked potatoes, mashed
1 tsp salt
1 tsp baking powder
225g/8oz plain flour
Pepper
60g/2oz butter, margarine or bacon fat
Milk

---

1. Peel and grate the raw potatoes. Wrap them tightly in a cloth and squeeze over a bowl to extract as much of the starch liquid as possible.

2. Thoroughly blend the grated raw potato into the cooked mashed potato.

3. Pour the liquid off the bowl of potato starch and scrape the starch into the potato mixture. Sift the salt and baking powder with the flour and add to the potatoes, mixing well.

4. Melt fat, add to the potatoes and mix again. Add as much milk as necessary to make the mixture into a batter of dropping consistency and season with pepper.

5. Heat some more fat on a griddle or in a heavy-based frying pan. When foaming drop in tablespoons of the batter.

6. Cook the pancakes in batches for 3-4 minutes on each side or until crispy and golden. Keep warm under a grill until all are cooked.

Aloo Mattar

SERVES 4-6

This Indian recipe is a semi-moist dish which blends easily with meat, chicken or fish curries.

PREPARATION: 10-15 mins
COOKING: 25-30 mins

60ml/4 tbsps cooking oil
1 medium-sized onion, finely chopped
2 cinnamon sticks, broken up
1.25cm/½-inch cube of root ginger, peeled and
    finely chopped
½ tsp ground turmeric
2 tsps ground cumin
¼ tsp chilli powder
¼ tsp freshly ground black pepper
460g/1lb potatoes, peeled and cut into 2.5cm/
    1-inch cubes
1-2 whole fresh green chillies
1 tbsp tomato purée
1 tsp salt or to taste
225ml/8 fl oz warm water
120g/4oz frozen garden peas
1 tbsp chopped coriander leaves

1. Heat the oil over a medium heat and fry the onion, cinnamon and ginger for 4-5 minutes, stirring frequently.

2. Reduce heat to low and add the turmeric, cumin, chilli powder and black pepper. Stir and fry for 1 minute.

3. Add the potatoes and chillies, stir and cook for 2-5 minutes until the spices are blended thoroughly. Stir in the tomato purée and salt.

4. Add the water, bring to the boil, cover the pan and cook over a medium to low heat for about 10 minutes until the potatoes are half cooked.

5. Add the peas, cover the pan and cook until the potatoes are tender.

6. Remove the pan from the heat, stir in half the coriander leaves and sprinkle the remainder on top.

Potato Pierozki

SERVES 6-8

These Polish dumplings are fried and served as a side dish to meat.

PREPARATION: 30 minutes, plus chilling
COOKING: 8 minutes, per batch

Dough
225g/8oz plain flour
Pinch salt
150g/5oz butter or margarine
1 egg
1 tbsp soured cream

Filling
30g/1oz butter
1 small onion, finely chopped
460g/1lb cooked potatoes, mashed
2 egg yolks
Salt and pepper

Oil for frying
Soured cream, to serve

1. First prepare the Pierozki dough. Sift the flour with a pinch of salt into a large bowl. Cut the butter into small pieces and rub into the flour until the mixture resembles fine breadcrumbs.

2. Mix the egg and soured cream together and combine with the flour and butter to make a firm dough. Knead the dough together quickly in the bowl, wrap well and chill for 30 minutes.

3. To prepare the filling, melt the butter in a small frying pan and sauté the onion for 3-4 minutes until softened. Combine with the

Step 6 Drop the filled and sealed Pierozki into boiling water and cook until they float to the surface.

potatoes and egg yolks and season well.

4. Roll the dough out very thinly on a well-floured surface and cut into circles about 7.5cm/3-inches in diameter.

5. Place teaspoons of the filling on to the dough circles and moisten the edges with water. Fold over the top and seal the edges well, crimping with a fork if wished.

6. To cook the Pierozki, drop a few at a time into boiling water. Simmer for 2-3 minutes or until they float to the top. Lift out of the water with a slotted spoon and drain on kitchen paper.

7. When all the Pierozki are done, heat about 60ml/4 tbsps oil in a frying pan and cook the Pierozki over brisk heat for about 3-4 minutes, or until lightly browned on both sides. Place the Pierozki on a serving plate and top with soured cream.

Index